This book belongs to

....

To my husband, Tim, and to saying, "Yes"

First published in Great Britain in 2024

Published by SPCK Children's
www.spckpublishing.co.uk
Part of the SPCK Group
Studio 101, The Record Hall, 16–16A Baldwin's Gardens, London EC1N 7RJ

Text copyright © Shell Perris 2024
Illustrations by Kathryn Wanless
This edition © The Society for Promoting Christian Knowledge 2024

Shell Perris has asserted her right under the Copyright, Designs and Patents Act, 1988,
to be identified as Author of this work.

British Library Cataloguing-in-Publication Data
A catalogue record for this book is available from the British Library

ISBN 978 0 281 08811 9

1 3 5 7 9 10 8 6 4 2

First printed in China by Dream Colour (Hong Kong) Printing Ltd

Produced on paper from sustainable sources

God's Promises for Everyone

spck

Written by
Shell Perris

Illustrated by
Kathryn Wanless

Contents

God's promises never fail...

The promises of God are forever unfailing.
They are for everyone – past, present, and future,
stamped with an everlasting seal that can never be broken.

Based on Joshua 21:45

You were created by God...

Every part of you has been lovingly made by God.
He knows everything about you, even the bits you choose to hide.
God looks at you and smiles.

Based on Psalm 139:13–14

God will always love you...

You can be near, or you can go far,
but you will never escape God's love for you.
It goes on and on, forever and always.

Based on Romans 8:38–39

God's arms are always open...

You don't have to be perfect or have all the answers.
Whatever you're going through, wherever you've been,
you can be sure that God will always welcome you into his arms.

Based on Ephesians 3:12

God has a plan for your life...

If you've ever wondered who made you,
it was God, and you are part of his plan.
You were thought of before the world began.

Based on Jeremiah 29:11

God will give you strength...

When you feel weak, God will be your source of strength.
There is no obstacle you cannot overcome
and no storm you cannot survive with God by your side.

Based on Isaiah 41:10

You are part of God's family...

Made by the same pair of hands, everyone has a place
in God's family, as sons and daughters of the King.
God calls you his child because he loves you.

Based on Ephesians 1:5

God will comfort you

when you are sad...

When sadness surrounds you and all you can do is cry,
know that God will hold you and share your sorrow.
Happiness is on the horizon.

Based on Matthew 5:4

Faith in God makes anything possible...

There is a mystery to God that is not meant to be discovered.
God will give us faith to believe in what we cannot see.
The smallest amount of faith makes mountains move.

Based on Matthew 17:20

With God,

you don't have to worry...

You are too precious to be carrying such heavy loads.
Pack up your worries and give them to God.
A still and thankful heart is much lighter.

Based on 1 Peter 5:7

God will be your guide...

God always knows the best way to go.
There is a lifetime of adventures just waiting to be had.
Hold on to God's hand and he will guide you.

Based on Psalm 32:8

God will
show you
what's right...

When you have that "gut feeling", it's likely to be God.
Listen carefully. He will gently reveal his ways
and teach you right from wrong.

Based on Proverbs 3:11–12

When you are tempted,
God will give you a way out...

When you are tempted to do something wrong
and you feel as if you want to give in,
God will give you the power to stay strong.

Based on 1 Corinthians 10:13

God will forgive you...

No one is perfect, except Jesus!
We all make mistakes every day.
If you say sorry to God and mean it,
he will forgive you and forget it ever happened.

Based on 1 John 1:9

God will be your
hiding place...

God will keep you safe from trouble and harm;
his presence is a hiding place, somewhere calm,
where unending love is found.

Based on Psalm 32:7

God will give you the desires of your heart...

God will place dreams and desires into your heart.
They are like heavenly songs waiting to be sung.
In God's timing, they will become anthems.

Based on Psalm 37:4

God will help you to keep going...

Sometimes, things happen that cause pain and sadness.
God won't stop them from happening, but he will pick you up,
dust you down, and help you to be brave.

Based on John 16:33

God's word will last forever...

Flowers flourish but fade over time;
leaves wither and fall to the ground.
But the word of God is forever alive and true,
lighting the fire inside of you.

Based on Isaiah 40:8

God will listen

when you pray...

When you talk to God, he listens and hears every word.
Whatever you're feeling, he feels it too.
God understands, even when others don't.

Based on 1 John 5:14–15

God rules over everything...

Nothing is beyond or bigger than God.
From the tiniest particle to the farthest galaxy,
God is the everlasting King and Ruler of all.

Based on Psalm 103:19

God is always good...

In a world where bad things can happen,
God stands up to the darkness with light.
He's God, he's good, and he can be trusted.

Based on Psalm 145:9

God will give you everything you need...

God knows what you need before you know you need it.

He has an endless supply of good things.

God will give generously at the right time.

Based on Philippians 4:19

God will never let you down...

When you are in a hopeless valley
and there seems to be no way out,
God will hold your hand, cheer you on, and walk beside you
as you climb to the next peak.

Based on Isaiah 43:2

God will bless you...

Whether you own much or have little, be thankful,
because what you do have is a pocket full of God's blessings.
Use them to bless others.

Based on 2 Corinthians 9:8

God can be trusted...

God can be trusted to do what he says he will do.
It might not always happen in the way we would like it to,
but God's ways are higher and greater than ours.

Based on Proverbs 3:5–6

God is always with you...

Wherever you go, God is with you.
He won't leave you all on your own.
Have courage – God is always enough.

Based on Joshua 1:9

God will protect you and keep you safe...

God is like an invisible forcefield, keeping you safe
from the fiery arrows of pain and sorrow that come your way.
He will guard you and strengthen you.

Based on 2 Thessalonians 3:3

Look for God

and you
will find him...

God can be found in all kinds of places:
in people and paintings, in the beauty of creation.
Keep searching and you will always find him.

Based on Matthew 7:7-8

God will take care of you...

God deeply cares for all, young and old, rich and poor.
You're lovingly made and incredibly loved.
God will carry you in his arms forever.

Based on Isaiah 46:4

God will fight for you...

When you can't, God can.
He will rise up in your place and fight for you.
Be at peace, for the victory has already been won.

Based on Exodus 14:14

If you believe
in Jesus,
God will save you...

Shout it from the rooftops, sing it in your heart,
"Jesus is King! He's not dead, he's alive!"
Then you will be rescued, released, and set free
from everything that holds you back from him.

Based on Romans 10:9

God will give you courage...

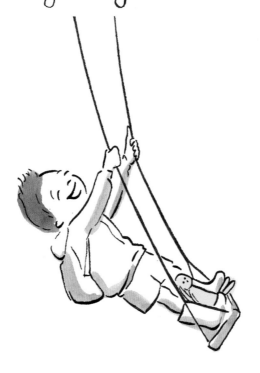

Don't be afraid of being bold and fearless.
God's power and love within you will put an end to fear
and cause courage to soar.

Based on 2 Timothy 1:7

God will be your source of hope...

The hope that God promises causes us to look up, keep going and fix our eyes on something far greater than the troubles we face. God's hope is freeing and endless.

Based on Isaiah 40:31

God will give you wisdom...

Sometimes, life is hard to understand. Everyone has questions.
Ask God for wisdom and things will become clear.
You'll know exactly what to do.

Based on James 1:5

God will never change...

Things change, people change, but God stays the same.
Like a rollercoaster, life will hold twists and turns, highs and lows,
but God is steady, constant, and unchanging – a firm foundation.

Based on Malachi 3:6

True joy is found in God...

Joy is like a strong tower that keeps you steady.
It's like sunshine on a rainy day. Spend time with God
and he will give you true, inner joy that goes far beyond feelings.

Based on Psalm 16:11

God's truth will set you free...

Don't believe the lies of this world.
You'll end up trapped, stuck, held back. Believe in God,
and the truth of his love will launch you into freedom.

Based on John 8:32

God will heal

the brokenhearted...

When you feel as if your heart is broken because of something or someone,
God will mend it with his comfort and love.
In time, your heart will feel whole once again.

Based on Psalm 147:3

God will give you rest...

Don't wait until you've got nothing left to give.
Rest in the palm of God's hand
and he will keep you from becoming worn out.
He will re-light and remind you of his fire in your soul.

Based on Matthew 11:28

God will help you
in times of trouble...

Trouble will play a part in life.
But, like a heroic knight, God will come to your rescue.
He will protect you with the sword and shield of his powerful presence.

Based on Psalm 46:1

God will make a way...

When it feels as if you've reached a dead end
or you've lost your way in life, God's light will shine
and reveal miraculous pathways you never knew existed.

Based on Isaiah 42:16

God will give you peace...

A cool, gentle breeze, a flickering candle, the soothing sway of the ocean.
God will give you a peace that is far greater than all these things.
Receive it, breathe it in, and be amazed!

Based on John 14:27

God will never turn you away...

Whoever you are, whatever you've done,
God will always welcome you with open arms. Run to him,
and he will be there to swoop you up and spin you around.

Based on John 6:37

God will help you to tell others about him...

The way you live and the choices you make speak louder than words alone.
God will help you to use every bit of your life
to show the world how wonderful he is.

Based on Matthew 28:19–20

God will do great things through you...

God is great and so are you.
When your heart is home to God, there is nothing you cannot do.
So, do great things with God and see how the world is changed.

Based on John 14:12

One day, God will put an end to all suffering...

There is a place where every heart is happy, every mind is free,
every body is new and every soul is revived.
Love God and have unlimited life forevermore.

Based on Revelation 21:4

Jesus will return...

Home, for Jesus, is the kingdom of heaven.
One day, when we're not expecting it,
this world will be dazzled by his presence once again.
Heaven will be our home, too.

Based on John 14:3

One day, you will be like Jesus...

Today, you may not be able to see God clearly,
but a day will come when you will.
On that day, you will shine brightly, just like Jesus.

Based on 1 John 3:2

God's light outshines the darkness...

When darkness is all around you, do not be afraid.
Jesus is the light of the world.
Even the smallest flicker of light chases the darkness away.

Based on John 8:12

God will be your friend forever...

If you want to be friends with God, all you need to say is, "Yes!"
"Yes, Jesus, I know you love me. Yes, Jesus, I've made mistakes.
You died on the cross because you love me so much
that you gave your life in place of mine."

Based on John 3:16

Index of Bible verses

The Old Testament

The New Testament